cheesecakes

THE AUSTRALIAN Women's Weekly

contents

Baked or chilled, light or decadent, classic or stylish café slices: what's not to love about cheesecakes? They may have been the height of sophistication during the seventies, but because they combine so well with the foods we love best – chocolate, berries, nuts – they've never gone out of fashion. Now is the time to rekindle your love affair with cheesecakes.

Editorial & Food Director

Australian cup and spoon measurements are metric. A conversion chart appears on page 77.

baked

If a baked cheesecake develops a crack, it could be that it was baked at too high a temperature. The filling should still have a bit of a wobble in the centre...it will firm up on cooling.

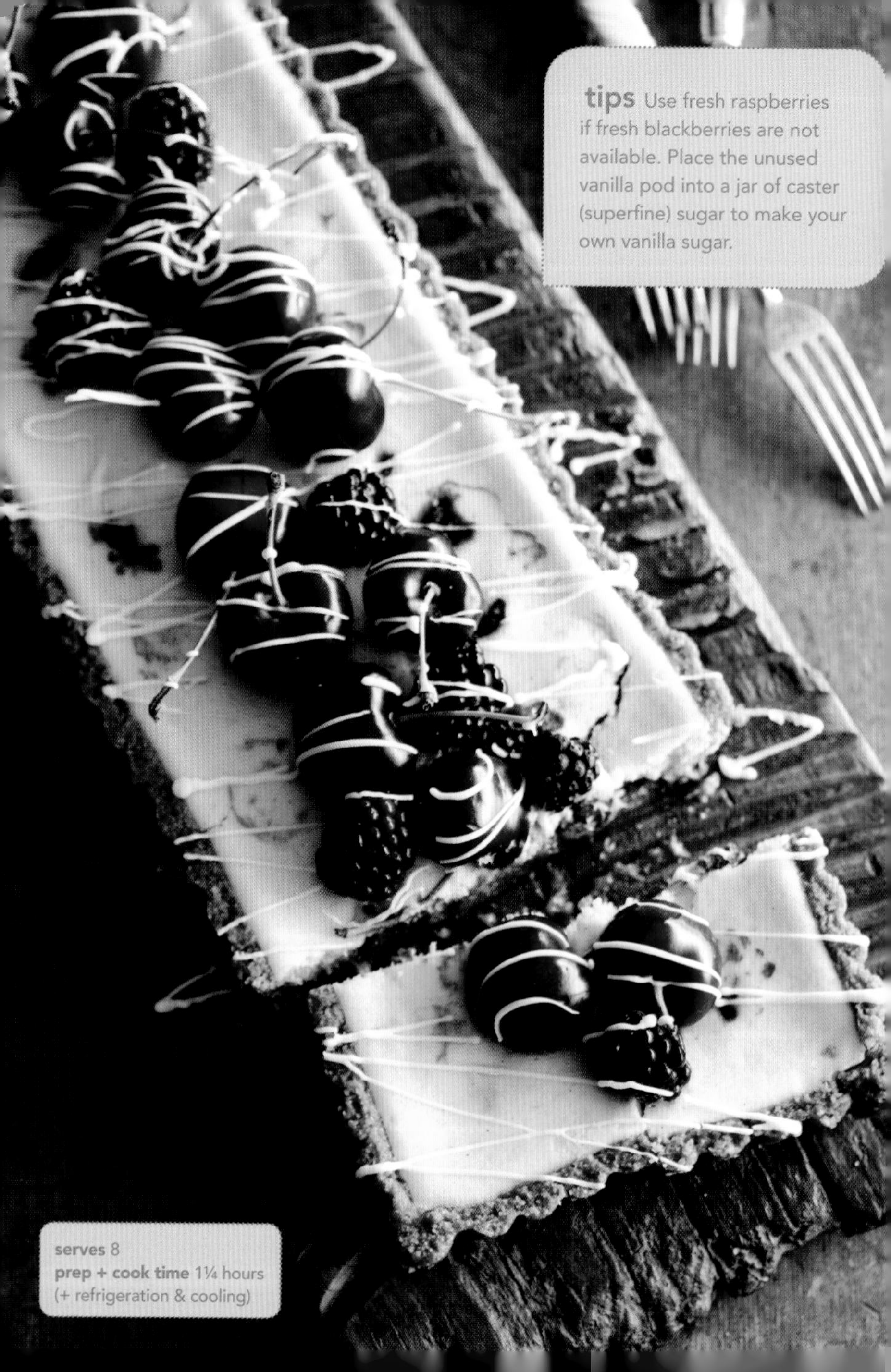

tips Use fresh raspberries if fresh blackberries are not available. Place the unused vanilla pod into a jar of caster (superfine) sugar to make your own vanilla sugar.

serves 8
prep + cook time 1¼ hours
(+ refrigeration & cooling)

cherry, blackberry & white chocolate cheesecake

- 250g (8 ounces) butternut snap biscuits
- 80g (2½ ounces) butter, melted
- 120g (4 ounces) white chocolate
- 1 vanilla bean, split lengthways
- 125g (4 ounces) cream cheese, softened
- ¼ cup (55g) caster (superfine) sugar
- 2 eggs
- ½ cup (125ml) pouring cream
- 100g (3 ounces) fresh cherries, seeded
- 100g (3 ounces) fresh blackberries
- 60g (2 ounces) white chocolate, extra
- 100g (3 ounces) fresh cherries, extra
- 100g (3 ounces) fresh blackberries, extra

1 Grease a 12.5cm x 35cm (5-inch x 14-inch) loose-based flan pan.

2 Process biscuits until fine. Add butter; process until combined. Press mixture over base and sides of flan pan. Place on an oven tray; refrigerate 30 minutes.

3 Preheat oven to 150°C/300°F.

4 Melt chocolate (see glossary entry, *chocolate, how to melt*, page 74). Cool slightly.

5 Scrape seeds from vanilla bean (keep pod for another use, see tips). Beat cream cheese, sugar, eggs and vanilla seeds in a small bowl with an electric mixer until thick and smooth.

6 Add cooled melted chocolate and the cream to cream cheese mixture; beat until thickens slightly. Pour filling over biscuit base; sprinkle with cherries and berries.

7 Bake cheesecake for 30 minutes or until just set. Cool in oven with door ajar. Cover; refrigerate 2 hours.

8 Just before serving, melt extra chocolate; cool slightly. Top cheesecake with extra fruit, drizzle with chocolate.

chocolate cheesecakes with caramel cream

- **½ cup (125ml) milk**
- **2 teaspoons white vinegar**
- **80g (2½ ounces) butter, softened**
- **2 eggs**
- **1 teaspoon vanilla extract**
- **⅔ cup (150g) caster (superfine) sugar**
- **1 cup (150g) plain (all-purpose) flour**
- **¼ cup (25g) cocoa powder**
- **½ teaspoon bicarbonate of soda (baking soda)**

cream cheese topping

- **250g (8 ounces) cream cheese, softened**
- **1 egg**
- **1 teaspoon vanilla extract**
- **⅓ cup (75g) caster (superfine) sugar**

caramel cream

- **60g (2 ounces) butter**
- **½ cup (110g) firmly packed brown sugar**
- **300ml (½ pint) thickened (heavy) cream**

1 Preheat oven to 180°C/350°F. Grease eight holes of a 12-hole (¾-cup/180ml) loose-based cheesecake pan.

2 Combine milk and vinegar in a jug. Beat butter, eggs, extract, caster sugar, sifted dry ingredients and milk mixture in a small bowl with an electric mixer on low speed until combined. Increase the speed to medium; beat 2 minutes or until mixture changes to a paler colour. Divide mixture into prepared pan holes. Bake 10 minutes.

3 Meanwhile, make cream cheese topping.

4 Remove cakes from oven. Divide topping among cakes, return to oven. Bake cakes for a further 10 minutes or until topping is barely set; cool in pan.

5 Meanwhile, make caramel cream.

6 Serve warm cakes with caramel cream. Dust with a little extra sifted cocoa powder and, if you like, top with chocolate shapes just before serving.

cream cheese topping Beat ingredients in a small bowl with an electric mixer until smooth and combined.

caramel cream Combine butter, sugar and ¼ cup of the cream in a small saucepan. Stir over high heat until smooth. Bring to the boil. Reduce heat; simmer, uncovered, for 3 minutes. Transfer to a medium heatproof bowl; cool to room temperature. Beat remaining cream in a small bowl with an electric mixer until soft peaks form. Swirl caramel through cream.

chocolate shapes Melt 50g (1½ ounces) dark chocolate (see glossary entry, *chocolate, how to melt*, page 74); place into a resealable plastic bag. Cut a tiny snip off one corner, and pipe small shapes onto baking paper. Leave shapes to set at room temperature.

tip A cheesecake pan is similar to a texas muffin pan, only the base is removable.

makes 8
prep + cook time
50 minutes (+ cooling)

tip Myzithra is a whey cheese traditionally produced on the island of Crete. If you can't find it, substitute mascarpone or ricotta.

cheesecake with brandied muscatels

- **125g (4 ounces) sponge finger biscuits (savoiardi)**
- **50g (1½ ounces) unsalted butter, melted**
- **500g (1 pound) unsalted fresh myzithra cheese**
- **½ cup (80g) icing (confectioners') sugar**
- **1 tablespoon finely grated lemon rind**
- **1 tablespoon cornflour (cornstarch)**
- **4 eggs**
- **½ cup (125ml) thickened (heavy) cream**
- **2 tablespoons flaked almonds, chopped coarsely**

brandied muscatels

- **¾ cup (165g) firmly packed brown sugar**
- **¼ cup (60ml) water**
- **¼ cup (60ml) brandy**
- **1 tablespoon honey**
- **12 small clusters muscatels**

serves 12
prep + cook time 1¾ hours (+ refrigeration & cooling)

1 Preheat oven to 140°C/280°F. Grease a 20cm (8-inch) round springform pan; line base and side with baking paper.

2 Process biscuits until fine. Add butter; process until combined. Press mixture firmly over base of pan. Place on an oven tray; refrigerate for 30 minutes.

3 Meanwhile, beat cheese, sifted icing sugar, rind and cornflour in a small bowl with an electric mixer until smooth. Beat in eggs, one at a time. Beat in cream, in two batches. Pour mixture into pan; sprinkle with nuts.

4 Bake cheesecake for 1¼ hours or until just set. Cool in oven with door ajar. Cover; refrigerate 1 hour.

5 Meanwhile, make brandied muscatels.

6 Serve cheesecake topped with muscatels and drizzled with syrup.

brandied muscatels

Stir sugar, the water, brandy and honey in a small saucepan over heat until sugar dissolves; bring to the boil. Reduce heat; simmer, uncovered, without stirring, about 5 minutes or until thickened slightly. Add muscatels; cool.

sour cream cheesecake

- **375g (12 ounces) plain sweet biscuits, halved**
- **185g (6 ounces) butter, melted**
- **250g (8 ounces) cottage cheese**
- **250g (8 ounces) cream cheese, softened**
- **2 teaspoons finely grated lemon rind**
- **¾ cup (165g) caster (superfine) sugar**
- **3 eggs**
- **1 cup (240g) sour cream**
- **¼ cup (60ml) lemon juice**
- **300g (9½ ounces) fresh blueberries**
- **2 teaspoons icing (confectioners') sugar**

1 Process biscuits until fine. Add butter; process until combined. Press mixture over base and side of a 22cm (9-inch) closed springform pan, stopping 5mm (¼-inch) from the top. Place on an oven tray; refrigerate 30 minutes.

2 Preheat oven to 160°C/325°F.

3 Push cottage cheese through a sieve into the medium bowl of an electric mixer. Add cream cheese, rind and sugar; beat with electric mixer until smooth. Beat in eggs, one at a time, then sour cream and juice. Pour mixture into pan.

4 Bake cheesecake for 1 hour or until just set. Cool in oven with door ajar. Cover; refrigerate 3 hours or overnight.

5 Top cheesecake with blueberries and dust with sifted icing sugar before serving.

serves 12
prep + cook time 1¾ hours
(+ refrigeration & cooling)

tip It's important to measure the springform pan when it's closed; the measurement appearing on the base of the pan sometimes refers to the measurement of the pan when it's open.

tips The cheesecake will sink slightly in the centre during baking. Store the cheesecake in an airtight container at room temperature for 1 day, or refrigerate for 1 week.

serves 16
prep + cook time 1¾ hours (+ refrigeration, cooling & standing)

wickedly rich butterscotch cheesecake

- **350g (11 ounces) dark (semi-sweet) chocolate block, softened slightly**
- **100g (3 ounces) butter, chopped**
- **⅔ cup (150g) firmly packed brown sugar**
- **4 eggs**
- **1 cup (150g) plain (all-purpose) flour**
- **500g (1 pound) cream cheese, softened**
- **2 teaspoons vanilla extract**
- **¾ cup (165g) caster (superfine) sugar**
- **1¼ cups (300g) sour cream**

butterscotch

- **200g (6½ ounces) butter, chopped**
- **1 cup (220g) firmly packed brown sugar**
- **300ml (½ pint) thickened (heavy) cream**

1 Make butterscotch.
2 Preheat oven to 150°C/300°F. Grease a 22cm (9-inch) closed springform pan; line base with baking paper.
3 Drag a large sharp knife across the back of the chocolate block to make large curls. You will need 100g (3 ounces) of chocolate curls. Place the curls in an airtight container; keep at room temperature for serving. Chop 100g (3 ounces) of the remaining chocolate coarsely; reserve.
4 Combine the last 150g (5 ounces) chocolate and butter in a small saucepan; stir over low heat until smooth. Transfer to a medium bowl and cool for 5 minutes. Stir brown sugar and one of the eggs into chocolate mixture; stir in sifted flour.
5 Spread mixture into pan. Place on an oven tray; bake brownie base for 15 minutes.
6 Meanwhile, beat cream cheese, extract and caster sugar in a small bowl with an electric mixer until combined. Beat in the remaining eggs, one at a time; beat in sour cream until combined. Pour half the cream cheese mixture over brownie base, drizzle with half the butterscotch; gently swirl through the mixture. Sprinkle with half the reserved chopped chocolate. Repeat layers.
7 Bake cheesecake for 45 minutes or until barely set in the centre. Cool in oven with door ajar. Cover; refrigerate about 4 hours or until firm.
8 Stand cheesecake at room temperature for 1 hour before serving. Top cheesecake with chocolate curls. Heat reserved butterscotch in a small saucepan; serve with cheesecake.

butterscotch Combine ingredients in a medium saucepan; stir over low heat until smooth. Simmer, uncovered, 3 minutes. Reserve 1½ cups for serving; transfer the remaining mixture into a small heatproof bowl. Refrigerate both mixtures.

tip We used a mixture of Shredded Wheatmeal biscuits and Morning Coffee biscuits for this crust (half the amount of each).

baked cheesecake with liqueur cherries

- **180g (5½ ounces) plain sweet biscuits**
- **125g (4 ounces) butter, melted**
- **500g (1 pound) cream cheese, softened**
- **250g mascarpone cheese, softened**
- **1 cup (220g) caster (superfine) sugar**
- **2 teaspoons finely grated lemon rind**
- **2 teaspoons vanilla extract**
- **3 eggs**

liqueur cherries

- **300g (9½ ounces) frozen cherries**
- **2 tablespoons cherry-flavoured liqueur**
- **1 tablespoon water**
- **1 tablespoon caster (superfine) sugar**
- **1 teaspoon lemon juice**

1 Grease a 24cm (9-inch) closed springform pan; line base and sides with baking paper.
2 Process biscuits until fine. Add butter; process until combined. Press mixture over base of pan. Place on an oven tray; refrigerate 30 minutes.
3 Preheat oven to 200°C/425°F.
4 Bake crumb crust for 10 minutes; cool.
5 Reduce oven to 180°C/350°F.
6 Beat cream cheese, mascarpone, sugar, rind and extract in a medium bowl with an electric mixer until smooth. Beat in eggs, one at a time. Do not overbeat.
7 Pour filling into crust; bake for 50 minutes. Cool in oven with door ajar. Cover; refrigerate 3 hours or overnight.
8 Make liqueur cherries; drizzle over cheesecake before serving.

liqueur cherries Combine ingredients in a medium saucepan; bring to the boil. Reduce heat; simmer cherries about 10 minutes or until mixture is slightly thickened.

serves 12
prep + cook time 1¾ hours
(+ refrigeration & cooling)

tips Brazil nuts have a lovely flavour and go well with fig and orange. Buy the best quality cinnamon sticks (or quills) you can, as often so-called cinnamon is really cassia bark sticks or quills. The best quality cinnamon is available from specialised spice shops.

spiced fig and orange cheesecake

- **½ cup (80g) brazil nuts**
- **125g (4 ounces) plain sweet biscuits**
- **80g (2½ ounces) butter, melted**
- **1 cup (250ml) orange juice**
- **1¼ cups (250g) finely chopped dried figs**
- **pinch ground cloves**
- **1 cinnamon stick**
- **2 teaspoons icing (confectioners') sugar**

orange filling

- **250g (8 ounces) cream cheese, softened**
- **1 tablespoon finely grated orange rind**
- **¾ cup (165g) caster (superfine) sugar**
- **1 cup (250g) mascarpone cheese**
- **2 eggs, separated**

serves 12
prep + cook time 2 hours
(+ refrigeration & cooling)

1 Grease a 22cm (9-inch) closed springform pan.
2 Process nuts and biscuits until fine. Add butter; process until combined. Press mixture over base of pan. Place pan on an oven tray; refrigerate 30 minutes.
3 Preheat oven to 160°C/325°F.
4 Simmer juice, figs, cloves and cinnamon in a small saucepan, uncovered, for 10 minutes or until most of the juice has been absorbed. Discard the cinnamon stick. Spread fig mixture over crumb base in pan.
5 Meanwhile, make orange filling; pour over fig mixture.
6 Bake cheesecake for 1¼ hours or until just set. Cool in oven with door ajar. Cover; refrigerate cheesecake 3 hours or overnight.
7 Dust cheesecake with sifted icing sugar just before serving.

orange filling Beat cream cheese, rind and the sugar in a medium bowl with an electric mixer until the mixture is smooth. Add mascarpone and egg yolks; beat only until combined. Beat egg whites in a small bowl with an electric mixer until soft peaks form; fold into cream cheese mixture.

butterscotch pecan cheesecake

- 150g (4½ ounces) plain chocolate biscuits
- 50g (1½ ounces) butter, melted
- 500g (1 pound) cream cheese, softened
- 1 teaspoon vanilla extract
- ¾ cup (165g) caster (superfine) sugar
- 2 eggs
- 1 tablespoon plain (all-purpose) flour
- ½ cup (60g) finely chopped roasted pecans

butterscotch topping

- ⅓ cup (75g) firmly packed brown sugar
- 40g (1½ ounces) butter
- 1 tablespoon pouring cream

1 Grease a 20cm (8-inch) closed springform pan.
2 Process biscuits until fine. Add butter; process until combined. Press mixture over base of pan. Place pan on an oven tray; refrigerate 30 minutes.
3 Preheat oven to 160°C/325°F.
4 Beat cream cheese, extract and sugar in a medium bowl with an electric mixer until smooth; beat in eggs, one at a time, until just combined. Stir in flour and nuts. Pour mixture into pan.
5 Bake cheesecake for 45 minutes or until just set. Cool in oven with door ajar.
6 Make butterscotch topping.
7 Spread butterscotch topping over cheesecake. Refrigerate for 3 hours or overnight.

butterscotch topping
Stir ingredients in a small saucepan over low heat until smooth.

serves 10
prep + cook time 1¼ hours
(+ refrigeration & cooling)

italian ricotta cheesecake

- **90g (3 ounces) butter, softened**
- **¼ cup (55g) caster (superfine) sugar**
- **1 egg**
- **1¼ cups (185g) plain (all-purpose) flour**
- **¼ cup (35g) self-raising flour**

ricotta filling

- **1kg (2 pounds) ricotta**
- **1 tablespoon finely grated lemon rind**
- **¼ cup (60ml) lemon juice**
- **1 cup (220g) caster (superfine) sugar**
- **5 eggs**
- **¼ cup (40g) sultanas**
- **¼ cup (80g) finely chopped glacé fruit salad**

serves 16
prep + cook time 1¾ hours
(+ refrigeration & cooling)

1 Grease a 28cm (11¼-inch) closed springform pan.
2 Beat butter, sugar and egg in a small bowl with an electric mixer until combined. Stir in half the sifted flours; then work in remaining flours by hand.
3 Knead pastry lightly on a floured surface until smooth, wrap in plastic; refrigerate 30 minutes.
4 Press pastry over base of pan; prick with a fork. Place on an oven tray; refrigerate 30 minutes.
5 Preheat oven to 200°C/400°F.
6 Cover pastry with baking paper, fill with dried beans or rice; bake for 10 minutes. Remove paper and beans; bake a further 15 minutes or until browned lightly. Cool.
7 Reduce oven to 160°C/325°F.
8 Make ricotta filling.
9 Pour filling into pan; bake for 50 minutes or until just set. Cool in oven with door ajar. Cover; refrigerate 3 hours or overnight
10 Dust cheesecake with sifted icing sugar before serving, if you like.

ricotta filling Process ricotta, rind, juice, sugar and eggs until smooth; stir in fruit.

white chocolate and cranberry cheesecakes

- **100g (3 ounces) plain sweet biscuits**
- **50g (1½ ounces) butter, melted**
- **150g (4½ ounces) frozen cranberries**
- **50g (1½ ounce) white chocolate**

white chocolate filling

- **¼ cup (60ml) pouring cream**
- **130g (4 ounces) white chocolate, chopped coarsely**
- **375g (12 ounces) cream cheese, softened**
- **1 teaspoon finely grated orange rind**
- **½ cup (110g) caster (superfine) sugar**
- **1 egg**

makes 6
prep + cook time 1 hour
(+ refrigeration & cooling)

1 Line a 6-hole (¾-cup/180ml) texas muffin pan with paper cases.

2 Process biscuits until fine. Add butter; process until combined. Divide mixture among paper cases; press firmly over bases of pan holes. Refrigerate 30 minutes.

3 Preheat oven to 150°C/300°F.

4 Meanwhile, make white chocolate filling.

5 Divide filling among cases; sprinkle with cranberries.

6 Bake cheesecakes for 30 minutes or until just set. Cool in oven with door ajar. Cover; refrigerate 3 hours or overnight.

7 Melt chocolate (see glossary entry, *chocolate, how to melt*, page 74); drizzle over cheesecakes before serving.

white chocolate filling

Stir cream and chocolate in a small saucepan over low heat until smooth; cool slightly. Beat cream cheese, rind, sugar and egg in a small bowl with an electric mixer until smooth; stir in cooled chocolate mixture.

serves 14
prep + cook time 1¾ hours
(+ cooling & refrigeration)

cinnamon and apple cheesecake

- **1 sheet ready-rolled shortcrust pastry**
- **750g (1½ pounds) cream cheese, softened**
- **¾ cup (165g) caster (superfine) sugar**
- **1 teaspoon ground cinnamon**
- **3 eggs, separated**
- **¾ cup (180ml) pouring cream**
- **2 medium apples (300g), unpeeled**
- **1 tablespoon lemon juice**
- **1 tablespoon demerara sugar**

1 Preheat oven to 180°C/350°F. Grease a 24cm (9½-inch) closed springform pan.

2 Cut pastry into a 24cm (9½-inch) round, press into base of pan; prick well with a fork. Place pan on an oven tray; bake about 20 minutes or until browned lightly. Cool 5 minutes.

3 Beat cream cheese, caster sugar, cinnamon and egg yolks in a medium bowl with an electric mixer until smooth; beat in cream. Beat egg whites in a small bowl with an electric mixer until soft peaks form; fold into cream cheese mixture in two batches. Pour filling mixture into pan.

4 Thinly slice unpeeled apple; combine in a small bowl with juice. Arrange slices, slightly overlapping, over filling; sprinkle with demerara sugar.

5 Bake cheesecake for 50 minutes. Cool in oven with door ajar. Cover; refrigerate 3 hours or overnight.

new york cheesecake

- **250g (8 ounces) plain sweet biscuits**
- **125g (4 ounces) butter, melted**
- **750g (1½ pounds) cream cheese, softened**
- **2 teaspoons finely grated orange rind**
- **1 teaspoon finely grated lemon rind**
- **1 cup (220g) caster (superfine) sugar**
- **3 eggs**
- **¾ cup (180g) sour cream**
- **¼ cup (60ml) lemon juice**

sour cream topping

- **1 cup (240g) sour cream**
- **2 tablespoons caster (superfine) sugar**
- **2 teaspoons lemon juice**

1 Grease a 24cm (9½-inch) closed springform pan.

2 Process biscuits until fine. Add butter; process until combined. Press mixture over base and side of pan. Place on an oven tray; refrigerate 30 minutes.

3 Preheat oven to 180°C/350°F.

4 Beat cream cheese, rinds and sugar in a medium bowl with an electric mixer until smooth. Beat in eggs, one at a time. Beat in sour cream and juice.

5 Pour filling into pan; bake 1¼ hours. Remove from oven; cool for 15 minutes.

6 Make sour cream topping. Spread over cheesecake; bake for 20 minutes or until just set. Cool in oven with door ajar. Cover; refrigerate 3 hours or overnight.

sour cream topping

Combine ingredients in a small bowl.

tip First produced in America in around 1872, cream cheese was developed by a dairy farmer trying to replicate the mild and creamy French cheese, Neufchâtel. However, by adding part cream and part milk to the mixture, he ended up creating cream cheese.

serves 12
prep + cook time 2½ hours
(+ refrigeration & cooling)

chilled

Chilled, or no-bake, cheesecakes use gelatine to set the filling; they are generally lighter in texture compared to baked ones. Fruits, berries, nuts and chocolate are favourite additions.

tips Redcurrant jelly is a preserve found in the jam section of large supermarkets. A cheesecake pan is similar to a texas muffin pan, only the base is removable.

makes 8
prep + cook time
45 minutes (+ refrigeration)

peach melba

- **200g (6½ ounces) shortbread biscuits**
- **90g (3 ounces) butter, melted**
- **1 teaspoon powdered gelatine**
- **1 tablespoon water**
- **250g (8 ounces) cream cheese**
- **⅓ cup (80ml) lemon juice**
- **2 tablespoons caster (superfine) sugar**
- **395g (12½ ounces) canned sweetened condensed milk**
- **1 teaspoon vanilla extract**
- **300ml (½ pint) thickened (heavy) cream**

poached peaches

- **1 cup (220g) caster (superfine) sugar**
- **2 cups (500ml) water**
- **4 medium peaches (600g)**

strawberry sauce

- **250g (8 ounces) strawberries, halved**
- **2 tablespoons caster (superfine) sugar**
- **2 tablespoons redcurrant jelly**
- **2 tablespoons water**

1 Grease 8 holes of a 12-hole (¾-cup/180ml) loose-based, straight-sided cheesecake pan.

2 Process biscuits until fine. Add butter; process until combined. Divide mixture evenly into pan holes, press firmly over base of pan using the bottom of a glass; refrigerate 20 minutes.

3 Add gelatine to the water in a small heatproof jug; stand jug in a small saucepan of simmering water. Stir until gelatine is dissolved. Cool.

4 Beat cream cheese, juice, sugar, condensed milk and extract in a small bowl with an electric mixer until smooth. Transfer to a large bowl; stir in gelatine mixture.

5 Beat cream in a small bowl with an electric mixer until soft peaks form; fold into cream cheese mixture. Spoon mixture into pan holes, smooth tops. Cover; refrigerate overnight.

6 Make poached peaches and strawberry sauce.

7 Remove cheesecakes from the pan; top with peaches and drizzle with sauce to serve.

poached peaches

Combine sugar and the water in a medium saucepan; stir over high heat, without boiling, until sugar dissolves. Simmer, uncovered, 2 minutes. Add whole peaches; simmer, uncovered, for about 10 minutes or until peaches are tender and skins start to come away. Remove peaches from liquid with a slotted spoon; cool. Peel away skins, halve peaches; discard stones. Cut peaches into wedges. Place peaches in a medium bowl; add ½ cup of the peach poaching liquid. Refrigerate 20 minutes.

strawberry sauce

Combine ingredients in a medium saucepan; stir, over low heat, until sugar dissolves. Simmer, uncovered, for about 5 minutes or until berries are soft. Push mixture through a fine sieve into a medium jug; discard any seeds.

lemon ricotta cheesecake

- **250g (8 ounces) ginger nut biscuits**
- **125g (4 ounces) butter, melted**
- **3 teaspoons powdered gelatine**
- **¼ cup (60ml) water**
- **300ml (½ pint) thickened (heavy) cream**
- **250g (8 ounces) cream cheese**
- **750g (1½ pounds) ricotta**
- **1 tablespoon finely grated lemon rind**
- **½ cup (110g) caster (superfine) sugar**
- **⅓ cup (80ml) lemon juice**

passionfruit topping

- **½ cup (125ml) orange juice**
- **2 tablespoons passionfruit pulp**
- **1 tablespoon caster (superfine) sugar**
- **2 teaspoons powdered gelatine**

1 Grease a 26cm (10½-inch) closed springform pan.

2 Process biscuits until fine. Add butter; process until combined. Press mixture over base of pan; refrigerate 30 minutes.

3 Add gelatine to the water in a small heatproof jug. Stand jug in a small saucepan of simmering water; stir until gelatine is dissolved. Cool.

4 Whip cream until soft peaks form. Beat cream cheese, ricotta, rind, sugar and juice in a large bowl with an electric mixer until smooth. Stir in gelatine mixture; fold in cream. Spread filling into pan; refrigerate overnight.

5 Make passionfruit topping; pour topping over cheesecake. Refrigerate until set.

passionfruit topping

Combine juice, pulp and sugar in a small saucepan; stir over low heat until sugar is dissolved. Remove from heat, add gelatine; stir until dissolved. Cool 15 minutes.

serves 16
prep + cook time
45 minutes (+ refrigeration)

double chocolate mousse cheesecake

- **125g (4 ounces) plain chocolate biscuits**
- **75g (2½ ounces) butter, melted**
- **3 teaspoons powdered gelatine**
- **¼ cup (60ml) water**
- **500g (1 pound) cream cheese, softened**
- **½ cup (110g) caster (superfine) sugar**
- **2 eggs, separated**
- **1 cup (250ml) pouring cream**
- **300g (9½ ounces) dark (semi-sweet) chocolate**
- **100g (3 ounces) white chocolate**
- **2 tablespoons pouring cream, extra**

serves 12
prep + cook time 1 hour (+ refrigeration)

1 Line a 22cm (9-inch) closed springform pan with plastic wrap.
2 Process biscuits until fine. Add butter; process until combined. Press mixture over base of pan. Refrigerate 30 minutes.
3 Add gelatine to the water in a small heatproof jug. Stand jug in a small saucepan of simmering water; stir until gelatine is dissolved. Cool.
4 Beat cream cheese, sugar and egg yolks in a medium bowl with an electric mixer until smooth; beat in cream. Melt half the dark chocolate (see glossary entry, *chocolate, how to melt*, page 74); stir chocolate and gelatine mixture into cream cheese mixture.
5 Beat egg whites in a small bowl with an electric mixer until soft peaks form; fold into cream cheese mixture, pour into pan.
6 Melt white chocolate. Combine white chocolate and extra cream in a small jug; swirl mixture through cheesecake mixture. Refrigerate overnight.
7 Melt remaining dark chocolate; spread over baking paper into a 20cm (8-inch) square. When set, break the chocolate into small pieces.
8 Remove cheesecake from pan; press chocolate pieces around side of cheesecake.

classic lemon cheesecake

- **250g (8 ounces) plain sweet biscuits**
- **125g (4 ounces) butter, melted**
- **1 teaspoon powdered gelatine**
- **1 tablespoon water**
- **250g (8 ounces) cream cheese, softened**
- **2 teaspoons finely grated lemon rind**
- **395g (12½ ounces) canned sweetened condensed milk**
- **⅓ cup (80ml) lemon juice**

lemon rind syrup

- **⅓ cup (75g) caster (superfine) sugar**
- **⅓ cup (80ml) water**
- **2 tablespoons shredded lemon rind**

1 Grease a 20cm (8-inch) closed springform pan.

2 Process biscuits until fine. Add butter; process until combined. Press mixture over base and side of pan; refrigerate 30 minutes.

3 Add gelatine to the water in a small heatproof jug. Stand jug in a small saucepan of simmering water; stir until gelatine is dissolved. Cool.

4 Beat cream cheese and rind in a small bowl with an electric mixer until smooth. Add condensed milk and juice; beat until mixture is smooth. Stir in gelatine mixture.

5 Pour filling into pan; refrigerate cheesecake overnight.

6 Make lemon rind syrup; drizzle over cheesecake to serve.

lemon rind syrup Stir sugar and the water in a small saucepan, over low heat, until sugar is dissolved. Simmer for 2 minutes, then add rind; simmer until syrup is thickened slightly; cool.

tip This classic cheesecake has a light lemon flavour but, for a flavour boost, infuse some fresh basil leaves in the syrup – remove the leaves before drizzling the syrup over the cheesecake.

serves 8
prep + cook time
30 minutes (+ refrigeration)

maple pecan cheesecake

- 185g (6 ounces) ginger nut biscuits
- 60g (2 ounces) butter, melted
- 3 teaspoons powdered gelatine
- ¼ cup (60ml) water
- 500g (1 pound) cream cheese, softened
- ⅓ cup (55g) firmly packed brown sugar
- 300ml (½ pint) pouring cream
- ½ cup (125ml) pure maple syrup

maple pecan topping

- 1¼ cups (175g) pecans, chopped coarsely
- 2 tablespoons pure maple syrup

makes 12
prep + cook time
45 minutes (+ refrigeration)

1 Grease a deep 19cm (8-inch) square cake pan; line base and sides with two sheets of baking paper, extending paper 5cm (2 inches) above sides of pan.
2 Process biscuits until fine. Add butter; process until combined. Press mixture over base of pan; refrigerate 30 minutes.
3 Add gelatine to the water in a small heatproof jug. Stand jug in a small saucepan of simmering water; stir until gelatine is dissolved. Cool.
4 Beat cream cheese and sugar in a medium bowl with an electric mixer until smooth; beat in cream and maple syrup. Stir in the gelatine mixture.
5 Pour filling into pan; refrigerate overnight.
6 Make maple pecan topping.
7 Serve cheesecake sprinkled with topping.

maple pecan topping
Preheat oven to 240°C/475°F. Combine nuts and maple syrup in a small bowl; spread mixture onto a greased oven tray. Roast for 10 minutes or until browned lightly; cool.

berry nougat cheesecake

- 125g (4 ounces) butternut snap biscuits
- 60g (2 ounces) butter, melted
- 100g (3 ounces) almond nougat, chopped finely
- 2 teaspoons powdered gelatine
- 2 tablespoons water
- 375g (12 ounces) cream cheese, softened
- ¼ cup (55g) caster (superfine) sugar
- 2 teaspoons lemon juice
- 300ml (½ pint) pouring cream
- 300g (9½ ounces) frozen raspberries

serves 10
prep + cook time
40 minutes (+ refrigeration)

1 Line a 22cm (9-inch) closed springform pan with plastic wrap.
2 Process biscuits until fine. Add butter; process until combined. Stir in the nougat. Press mixture over base of pan; refrigerate 30 minutes.
3 Add gelatine to the water in a small heatproof jug. Stand jug in a small saucepan of simmering water; stir until gelatine is dissolved. Cool.
4 Beat cream cheese, sugar and juice in a small bowl with an electric mixer until smooth; beat in cream, then stir in the gelatine mixture.
5 Sprinkle half the berries over base; spread with cream cheese mixture. Refrigerate overnight.
6 Blend or process remaining berries; strain and discard seeds. Serve cheesecake accompanied with berry purée.

tip Any frozen berry will work here; try blueberry, strawberry or blackberry, or use a mixture of berries.

baklava cheesecake

- **⅓ cup (35g) walnuts**
- **⅔ cup (90g) pistachios**
- **2 teaspoons mixed spice**
- **250g (8 ounces) butternut snap biscuits**
- **½ cup (70g) slivered almonds**
- **125g (4 ounces) unsalted butter**
- **3 teaspoons powdered gelatine**
- **¼ cup (60ml) water**
- **500g (1 pound) cream cheese, softened**
- **½ cup (110g) caster (superfine) sugar**
- **¼ cup (90g) honey**
- **1½ cups (375ml) thickened (heavy) cream**

1 Preheat oven to 220°C/425°F. Grease a 26cm (10½-inch) closed springform pan.

2 Roast walnuts and pistachios on an oven tray for about 5 minutes. Sprinkle nuts with spice; roast for 1 minute, cool. Process spiced nuts with biscuits until fine; transfer to a medium bowl, stir in almonds.

3 Meanwhile, melt butter; cool slightly.

4 Set aside one-third of the nut mixture. Stir butter into remaining nut mixture. Press mixture evenly over base of pan; refrigerate 30 minutes.

5 Add gelatine to the water in a small heatproof jug. Stand jug in a small saucepan of simmering water; stir until gelatine is dissolved. Cool.

6 Beat cream cheese, sugar and honey in a medium bowl with an electric mixer until smooth; beat in cream. Stir in gelatine mixture.

7 Pour cream cheese mixture into pan; sprinkle top with reserved nut mixture. Cover; refrigerate overnight.

serves 16
prep + cook time
35 minutes (+ refrigeration)

tiramisu cheesecake

- **¼ cup (20g) medium ground espresso coffee beans**
- **1 cup (250ml) boiling water**
- **2 tablespoons caster (superfine) sugar**
- **⅓ cup (80ml) marsala**
- **250g (8 ounces) sponge finger biscuits (savoiardi)**
- **2 teaspoons powdered gelatine**
- **2 tablespoons water, extra**
- **300ml (½ pint) thickened (heavy) cream**
- **125g (4 ounces) cream cheese, softened**
- **¼ cup (40g) icing (confectioners') sugar**
- **250g (8 ounces) mascarpone cheese**
- **2 tablespoons marsala, extra**
- **150g chocolate-coated coffee beans, chopped coarsely**

1 Grease a 24cm (9½-inch) closed springform pan.

2 Combine coffee and the water in a coffee plunger; stand 4 minutes before plunging. Combine coffee, caster sugar and marsala in a medium heatproof bowl; cool for 10 minutes.

3 Place ⅓ cup of the coffee mixture in a small saucepan; simmer, uncovered, until mixture is reduced to about 1 tablespoon. Cool.

4 Cut each biscuit into 7cm (2¾-inch) lengths; reserve end pieces. Dip flat side of biscuits, one at a time, in remaining coffee mixture; arrange biscuits, round-side out, around side of pan. Dip reserved biscuit ends in coffee mixture; place over base of pan.

5 Add gelatine to the extra water in a small heatproof jug. Stand jug in a small saucepan of simmering water; stir until gelatine is dissolved. Cool.

6 Whip cream until soft peaks form.

7 Beat cream cheese and sifted icing sugar in a medium bowl with an electric mixer until smooth. Add mascarpone and the extra marsala; beat until mixture is combined. Stir in the gelatine mixture; fold in whipped cream.

8 Spread filling into pan. Drizzle reduced coffee mixture over cheesecake, pull skewer backwards and forwards several times for a marbled effect. Refrigerate overnight.

9 Serve cheesecake topped with chocolate-coated coffee beans.

serves 12
prep + cook time 1 hour
(+ cooling & refrigeration)

tips You need an 80cm (32-inch) length of 50mm (2-inch) diameter PVC pipe, cut into 10cm (4-inch) lengths; ask the hardware store to do this for you. This recipe will also fit into a 24cm (9-inch) closed springform pan. In this case, use a plain chocolate biscuit base (see step 2, *double chocolate mousse cheesecake*, page 37).

cookies and cream cheesecakes

- **300g (9½ ounces) cream-filled chocolate biscuits**
- **2 teaspoons powdered gelatine**
- **2 tablespoons water**
- **180g (6 ounces) white chocolate**
- **375g (12 ounces) cream cheese, softened**
- **1 teaspoon vanilla extract**
- **½ cup (110g) caster (superfine) sugar**
- **300ml (½ pint) pouring cream**
- **50g (1½ ounces) dark (semi-sweet) chocolate**

1 Stand eight cleaned 10cm (4-inch) lengths of PVC pipes on a tray; grease each pipe and line with baking paper.
2 Place one biscuit in each pipe. Chop remaining biscuits into quarters.
3 Add gelatine to the water in a small heatproof jug. Stand jug in a small saucepan of simmering water; stir until gelatine is dissolved. Cool.
4 Melt white chocolate (see glossary entry, *chocolate, how to melt*, page 74); cool slightly.
5 Beat cream cheese, extract and sugar in a medium bowl with an electric mixer until smooth; beat in cream. Stir in melted white chocolate, gelatine mixture and reserved biscuits. Divide filling among pipes; refrigerate overnight.
6 Melt dark chocolate; cool slightly. Remove pipes and paper from cheesecakes; drizzle over the chocolate to serve.

makes 8
prep + cook time
35 minutes (+ refrigeration)

sticky rhubarb on citrus

- **250g (8 ounces) plain sweet biscuits**
- **125g (4 ounces) butter, melted**
- **¼ teaspoon ground nutmeg**
- **4 eggs, separated**
- **1 cup (220g) caster (superfine) sugar**
- **2 tablespoons finely grated lemon rind**
- **½ cup (125ml) lemon juice**
- **½ cup (125ml) orange juice**
- **1½ tablespoons powdered gelatine**
- **½ cup (125ml) water**
- **500g (1 pound) cream cheese, softened**
- **300ml (½ pint) thickened (heavy) cream**

sticky rhubarb

- **8 large stems trimmed rhubarb (500g), cut into 5cm (2-inch) lengths**
- **¾ cup (165g) caster (superfine) sugar**
- **2 teaspoons lemon juice**

makes 8
prep + cook time 1¼ hours (+ refrigeration)

1 Start making sticky rhubarb.
2 Grease eight 10cm (4-inch) round springform pans or a 28cm (11¼-inch) closed springform pan; place on a tray.
3 Process biscuits until fine. Add butter and nutmeg; process until combined. Press mixture over pan bases; refrigerate 30 minutes.
4 Combine egg yolks, sugar, rind and juices in a medium heatproof bowl; whisk over a medium saucepan of simmering water about 10 minutes or until thick and foamy. Remove from heat.
5 Sprinkle gelatine over the water in a small heatproof jug. Stand jug in a small saucepan of simmering water. Stir until gelatine dissolves; stir into egg yolk mixture. Cool.
6 Beat cream cheese in a large bowl with an electric mixer until smooth; beat in egg yolk mixture in four batches.
7 Whip cream until soft peaks form. Beat egg whites in a small bowl, with an electric mixer until soft peaks form. Fold whipped cream into cream cheese mixture, then fold in egg whites in two batches. Divide mixture among pans; refrigerate overnight.
8 Remove rhubarb mixture from refrigerator; continue making sticky rhubarb. Top cheesecakes with sticky rhubarb.

sticky rhubarb Combine rhubarb and sugar in a colander, stand colander in a bowl; refrigerate overnight. (Continue the next day from step 8.) Combine rhubarb and drained liquid in a large frying pan; simmer, uncovered for about 5 minutes or until the rhubarb has softened. Fold in juice; cool.

tip Any poached fruit will work here; but use something with a more robust flavour, stone fruits are a good choice.

tip We used Malibu, but use your favourite coconut-flavoured liqueur.

pineapple and coconut cheesecake

- 180g (5½ ounces) coconut macaroons
- 60g (2 ounces) butter, melted
- 1½ teaspoons powdered gelatine
- 2 tablespoons water
- 250g (8 ounces) cream cheese, softened
- ¼ cup (55g) caster (superfine) sugar
- 1 cup (250ml) pouring cream
- ¼ cup (60ml) coconut-flavoured liqueur

pineapple topping

- 1 cup (250ml) pineapple juice
- ¼ small pineapple (225g), halved lengthways, sliced thinly

makes 12
prep + cook time
35 minutes (+ refrigeration & cooling)

1 Grease a 12-hole (¼-cup/60ml) mini cheesecake pan with removable bases.
2 Process macaroons until fine. Add butter; process until combined. Press a heaped tablespoon of mixture over the base of each pan hole; refrigerate 30 minutes.
3 Add gelatine to the water in a small heatproof jug. Stand jug in a small saucepan of simmering water; stir until gelatine is dissolved. Cool.
4 Beat cream cheese and sugar in a small bowl with an electric mixer until smooth; beat in cream. Stir in liqueur and gelatine mixture. Divide mixture into pan holes; refrigerate overnight.
5 Make pineapple topping.
6 Serve cheesecakes topped with pineapple and thickened juices.

pineapple topping Combine juice and pineapple in a medium frying pan; simmer for about 10 minutes or until pineapple is soft. Remove pineapple from juice; simmer juice for about 5 minutes or until liquid thickens slightly. Cool.

mint chocolate truffle

- **125g (4 ounces) plain chocolate biscuits**
- **35g (1-ounce) Peppermint Crisp chocolate bar**
- **75g (2½ ounces) butter, melted**
- **2 teaspoons powdered gelatine**
- **2 tablespoons water**
- **1½ cups (375ml) thickened (heavy) cream**
- **500g (8 ounces) cream cheese, softened**
- **½ cup (110g) caster (superfine) sugar**
- **¼ cup (60ml) peppermint-flavoured liqueur**

truffles

- **2 tablespoons thickened (heavy) cream**
- **100g (3 ounces) dark (semi-sweet) chocolate, chopped coarsely**
- **2 x 35g (1-ounce) Peppermint Crisp chocolate bars, chopped finely**

makes 8
prep + cook time 1 hour
(+ refrigeration & cooling)

1 Make truffles.
2 Stand eight cleaned 10cm (4-inch) lengths of PVC pipes on a tray; grease each pipe and line with baking paper.
3 Process biscuits and chocolate bar until fine. Add butter; process until combined. Divide mixture among pipes; using the end of a wooden spoon, press mixture down evenly. Refrigerate 30 minutes.
4 Add gelatine to the water in a small heatproof jug. Stand jug in a small saucepan of simmering water; stir until gelatine is dissolved. Cool.
5 Whip cream until soft peaks form. Beat cream cheese and sugar in a medium bowl with an electric mixer until smooth. Stir in gelatine mixture and liqueur; fold in cream.
6 Divide filling evenly among pipes; refrigerate overnight.
7 Remove pipes and paper from cheesecakes. Serve topped with truffles and small fresh mint leaves, if you like.

truffles Combine cream and the chocolate in a small saucepan; stir over low heat until smooth. Transfer to a small bowl, cover; refrigerate 3 hours. Roll ½-teaspoonfuls of mixture into balls; place on a tray. Roll balls in Peppermint Crisp; return to tray. Refrigerate truffles until firm.

tip You need an 80cm (32-inch) length of 50mm (2-inch) diameter PVC pipe, cut into 10cm (4-inch) lengths; ask the hardware store to do this for you. This recipe will also fit into six 10cm (4-inch) springform pans or a 24cm (9½-inch) springform pan.

slices

These delicious slices are just the thing for afternoon snacks, tea parties and, because they can be made the day before, they're time-friendly treats for 'bring a plate' days with friends.

makes 18
prep + cook time 1½ hours
(+ standing, cooling & refrigeration)

double chocolate rum and raisin cheesecakes

- **150g (4½ ounces) butter, chopped coarsely**
- **100g (3 ounces) dark (semi-sweet) chocolate, chopped coarsely**
- **1 cup (220g) caster (superfine) sugar**
- **⅔ cup (160ml) water**
- **1 cup (150g) plain (all-purpose) flour**
- **2 tablespoons cocoa powder**
- **2 egg yolks**
- **1 tablespoon cocoa powder, extra**

rum and raisin filling

- **⅓ cup (80ml) dark rum**
- **1 cup (160g) coarsely chopped raisins**
- **250g (8 ounces) dark (semi-sweet) chocolate**
- **500g (1 pound) cream cheese, softened**
- **½ cup (110g) caster (superfine) sugar**
- **3 eggs**

1 Start making rum and raisin filling.

2 Preheat oven to 180°C/350°F. Grease a 20cm x 30cm (8-inch x 12-inch) lamington pan; line base with baking paper, extending paper 5cm (2 inches) above two long sides.

3 Stir butter, chocolate, sugar and the water in a medium saucepan over low heat until smooth. Remove from heat; stir in sifted flour and cocoa, then egg yolks. Pour mixture into pan; bake about 15 minutes. Cool in pan.

4 Meanwhile, continue making filling. Pour filling over base.

5 Bake cheesecake for 45 minutes or until just set. Cool in oven with door ajar. Refrigerate for 3 hours or overnight. Cut into squares; serve cheesecake dusted with extra cocoa.

rum and raisin filling
Combine rum and raisins in a small bowl. Cover; stand 3 hours. (Continue from step 4.) Melt the chocolate (see glossary entry, *chocolate, how to melt*, page 74); cool slightly. Beat cream cheese and sugar in a medium bowl with an electric mixer until smooth. Beat in eggs, one at a time. Stir in chocolate, then the rum and raisin mixture.

cheesecake brownies

- **125g (4 ounces) butter, chopped**
- **150g (4½ ounces) dark (semi-sweet) chocolate, chopped coarsely**
- **1 egg**
- **⅔ cup (150g) caster (superfine) sugar**
- **¾ cup (110g) plain (all-purpose) flour**
- **¼ cup (35g) self-raising flour**

cream cheese topping

- **250g (8 ounces) cream cheese, softened**
- **1 teaspoon vanilla extract**
- **⅓ cup (75g) caster (superfine) sugar**
- **1 egg**
- **½ cup (125ml) pouring cream**

1 Preheat oven to 180°C/350°F. Grease a deep 19cm (8-inch) square cake pan; line base and sides with baking paper, extending paper 5cm (2 inches) above sides of pan.

2 Stir the butter and chocolate in a small saucepan over low heat until smooth. Cool.

3 Beat egg and sugar in a small bowl with an electric mixer until thick and creamy. Stir in chocolate mixture and sifted flours. Spread mixture into pan; bake 10 minutes.

4 Make cream cheese topping; pour over brownie base.

5 Bake cheesecake for 15 minutes or until just set. Cool in oven with door ajar. Refrigerate 3 hours before serving.

cream cheese topping

Beat cream cheese, extract, sugar and egg in a small bowl with an electric mixer until smooth; beat in cream.

tips This versatile slice can be served cut (straight from the fridge) into small finger-lengths as a treat or, cut into squares and topped with fresh berries for a charming dessert. Or, for a more tart flavour, drizzle with passionfruit pulp.

makes 16
prep + cook time 1 hour
(+ cooling & refrigeration)

tip We used Digestive biscuits in this recipe, but you can use Graham Crackers or Shredded Wheatmeal biscuits.

caramel cheesecake slice

- **200g (6½ ounces) plain sweet biscuits**
- **½ cup (60g) pecans, roasted**
- **100g (3½ ounces) unsalted butter, melted**
- **380g (12 ounces) canned caramel top'n'fill**

cream cheese filling

- **500g (1 pound) cream cheese, softened**
- **2 teaspoons vanilla extract**
- **½ cup (110g) caster (superfine) sugar**
- **2 eggs**
- **1 cup (250ml) thickened (heavy) cream**

1 Grease a 20cm x 30cm (8-inch x 12-inch) rectangular slice pan; line the base and long sides with baking paper, extending paper 5cm (2 inches) over sides.
2 Process biscuits and nuts until fine. Add butter; process until combined. Press mixture evenly over base of pan; refrigerate 30 minutes.
3 Preheat oven to 140°C/280°F.
4 Make cream cheese filling.
5 Spread caramel over biscuit base; pour filling over caramel. Bake for 45 minutes or until just set. Cool in oven with door ajar. Refrigerate for 3 hours or overnight before cutting into small squares to serve.

cream cheese filling Beat cream cheese, extract, sugar and eggs in a medium bowl with an electric mixer until smooth. Gradually beat in cream.

makes 48
prep + cook time 1 hour
(+ refrigeration & cooling)

tip Cinnamon sugar is a combination of ground cinnamon and caster sugar; it is available in the supermarket spice section.

honey and spice slice

- **250g (8 ounces) ginger nut biscuits**
- **100g (3½ ounces) butter, melted**
- **500g (1 pound) cream cheese, softened**
- **¼ cup (55g) caster (superfine) sugar**
- **¼ cup (90g) honey**
- **1 teaspoon vanilla extract**
- **2 teaspoons mixed spice**
- **½ cup (125ml) pouring cream**
- **2 eggs, separated**
- **2 teaspoons cinnamon sugar**

1 Grease a 20cm x 30cm (8-inch x 12-inch) rectangular pan; line base and long sides with baking paper, extending paper 5cm (2 inches) over sides.

2 Process biscuits until fine. Add butter; process until combined. Press mixture over base of pan; refrigerate 30 minutes.

3 Preheat oven to 160°C/325°F.

4 Beat cream cheese, sugar, honey, extract and spice in a medium bowl with an electric mixer until smooth; beat in cream and egg yolks.

5 Beat egg whites in a small bowl with an electric mixer until soft peaks form; fold into cream cheese mixture.

6 Pour cream cheese mixture into pan; bake for 30 minutes or until just set. Cool in oven with door ajar. Refrigerate 3 hours or over overnight.

7 Sprinkle slice with cinnamon sugar before cutting into squares.

makes 20
prep + cook time 1 hour
(+ refrigeration & cooling)

makes 24
prep + cook time
20 minutes (+ refrigeration)

lemon cheesecake squares

- **250g (8 ounces) butternut snap biscuits**
- **½ cup (40g) flaked almonds**
- **125g (4 ounces) butter, melted**
- **250g (8 ounces) cream cheese, softened**
- **3 teaspoons finely grated lemon rind**
- **395g (12½ ounces) canned sweetened condensed milk**
- **⅓ cup (80ml) lemon juice**

1 Grease a 20cm x 30cm (8-inch x 12-inch) rectangular pan; line base and long sides with baking paper, extending paper 5cm (2 inches) over sides.

2 Process biscuits and nuts until fine. Add butter; process until combined. Press mixture over base of pan; refrigerate 30 minutes.

3 Beat cream cheese and rind in a medium bowl with an electric mixer until smooth. Add condensed milk and juice; beat until smooth. Pour cheese mixture over base. Refrigerate overnight before cutting.

jaffa liqueur squares

- **250g (8 ounces) plain chocolate biscuits**
- **150g (4½ ounces) butter, melted**

jaffa filling

- **100g (3 ounces) dark (semi-sweet) chocolate**
- **3 eggs**
- **¾ cup (165g) caster (superfine) sugar**
- **500g (1 pound) cream cheese, softened**
- **1 tablespoon finely grated orange rind**
- **2 tablespoons citrus-flavoured liqueur**

chocolate ganache

- **150g (4½ ounces) dark (semi-sweet) chocolate, chopped coarsely**
- **¼ cup (60ml) pouring cream**

makes 12
prep + cook time 1¼ hours (+ refrigeration & cooling)

1 Grease a 19cm x 29cm (8-inch x 12-inch) rectangular pan; line base with baking paper, extending paper 5cm (2 inches) over long sides.

2 Process biscuits until fine. Add butter; process until combined. Press mixture over base of pan; refrigerate 30 minutes.

3 Preheat oven to 160°C/325°F.

4 Make jaffa filling.

5 Pour both fillings into pan, swirl with a skewer; bake for 25 minutes or until just set. Cool in oven with door ajar.

6 Make chocolate ganache.

7 Spread ganache over cheesecake; refrigerate 3 hours or overnight.

jaffa filling Melt chocolate (see glossary entry, *chocolate, how to melt*, page 74); cool slightly. Beat eggs and sugar in a small bowl with an electric mixer until thick and creamy. Beat cream cheese in a medium bowl with an electric mixer until smooth; beat in egg mixture in two batches. Pour half the filling into another medium bowl. Stir cooled melted chocolate into one bowl, and rind and liqueur into the other bowl.

chocolate ganache Combine ingredients in a small saucepan; stir over low heat until smooth. Cool 10 minutes.

tip We used Cointreau, but you can use your favourite citrus-flavoured liqueur. Use orange juice instead of the liqueur, if you like.

mixed spice with honey syrup cheesecake

- **250g (8 ounces) plain sweet biscuits**
- **125g (4 ounces) butter, melted**

mixed spice filling

- **500g (1 pound) cream cheese, softened**
- **½ cup (110g) firmly packed brown sugar**
- **2 teaspoons vanilla extract**
- **1 teaspoon mixed spice**
- **½ cup (125ml) pouring cream**
- **3 egg yolks**
- **2 egg whites**

honey syrup

- **2 cinnamon sticks**
- **4 strips lemon rind**
- **⅓ cup (120g) honey**
- **1 tablespoon water**
- **¾ teaspoon powdered gelatine**

1 Grease a deep 19cm (8-inch) square cake pan; line base and sides with baking paper, extending paper 5cm (2 inches) above sides of pan.

2 Process biscuits until fine. Add butter; process until combined. Press mixture over base of pan; refrigerate 30 minutes.

3 Preheat oven to 160°C/325°F.

4 Make mixed spice filling.

5 Pour filling into pan; bake 50 minutes. Cool in oven with door ajar. Refrigerate cheesecake 3 hours or overnight.

6 Make honey syrup. Serve cheesecake with warm syrup.

mixed spice filling Beat cream cheese, sugar, extract and spice in a medium bowl with an electric mixer until smooth; beat in cream and egg yolks. Beat egg whites in a small bowl with an electric mixer until soft peaks form; fold into cream cheese mixture.

honey syrup Combine ingredients in a small saucepan, bring to the boil; remove from heat. Discard the cinnamon stick before serving.

makes 9
prep + cook time 1¼ hours (+ refrigeration & cooling)

black forest slice

- 425g (13½ ounces) canned seedless black cherries in syrup
- 200g (6½ ounces) dark (semi-sweet) chocolate
- 125g (4 ounces) cream cheese, softened
- 125g (4 ounces) mascarpone cheese
- ½ cup (110g) caster (superfine) sugar
- ⅔ cup (160ml) pouring cream
- 1 egg, separated

cherry topping

- 85g (3 ounces) packet cherry-flavoured jelly crystals
- ⅔ cup (160ml) boiling water

makes 8
prep + cook time 1¼ hours (+ cooling & refrigeration)

1 Drain cherries; reserve syrup. Make the topping.
2 Preheat oven to 160°C/325°F. Grease a 19cm x 29cm (8-inch x 12-inch) rectangular pan; line base with baking paper, extending paper 5cm (2 inches) over long sides.
3 Melt chocolate (see glossary entry, *chocolate, how to melt*, page 74); spread chocolate over base of pan, refrigerate until set.
4 Beat cream cheese, mascarpone, sugar, cream and egg yolk in a small bowl with an electric mixer until smooth; stir in cherries.
5 Beat egg white in a small bowl with an electric mixer until soft peaks form; fold into cream cheese mixture. Pour over chocolate base.
6 Bake 35 minutes. Cool in oven with door ajar.
7 Pour topping over cheesecake. Refrigerate overnight.

cherry topping Combine jelly crystals and the boiling water in a small bowl; stir until jelly is dissolved. Stir in ⅔ cup reserved cherry syrup; cool. Refrigerate jelly until thickened to the stage where it resembles unbeaten egg whites.

ALMOND a flat, pointy-ended nut with a pitted brown shell enclosing a creamy white kernel covered by a brown skin.
flaked paper-thin slices.
nougat a confectionery made from honey, almonds and egg whites. We are most familiar with the chewy white nougat studded with nuts, however, it can be either soft and chewy or crunchy.
slivered small lengthways-cut pieces.

BAKING PAPER also parchment paper or baking parchment – is a silicone-coated paper that is primarily used for lining baking pans and oven trays so cakes and biscuits won't stick making removal and cleaning easy.

BICARBONATE OF SODA also known as baking or carb soda; used as a raising agent in baking.

BISCUITS also known as cookies.
butternut snap a crunchy cookie made with golden syrup, oats and coconut.
coconut macaroons a sweet biscuit made with almonds, sugar and egg whites.
ginger nut a plain biscuit made with golden syrup and ginger.
shortbread a sweet pale golden, crumbly, buttery-tasting biscuit.
sponge finger also known as savoiardi, savoy biscuits, lady's fingers or sponge fingers; crisp fingers made with sponge-cake mixture.

BRAZIL NUT a triangular nut with a hard shell; has a white flesh encased with a brown skin.

BUTTER use salted or unsalted butter; 125g is equal to one stick, or 4 ounces, of butter.
unsalted butter, often called 'sweet' butter, simply has no added salt.

CHEESE
cottage fresh, white, unripened curd cheese with a grainy consistency.
cream commonly known as Philadelphia or Philly; a soft cows-milk cheese. Is the traditional cheese used in cheesecakes.
mascarpone a cultured cream product made in much the same way as yoghurt. It's whitish to creamy yellow in colour, with a soft, creamy texture.
myzithra traditionally made on the isle of Crete; fresh myzithra is a soft whey cheese similar to ricotta.
ricotta a sweet, moist cows-milk cheese with a slightly grainy texture.

CHOCOLATE
dark also semi-sweet or luxury chocolate; contains a high percentage of cocoa liquor and cocoa butter, and little added sugar.
milk the most popular eating chocolate, mild and very sweet; similar in make-up to dark with the difference being the addition of milk solids.
white contains no cocoa solids but derives its sweet flavour from cocoa butter. It is very sensitive to heat, so watch carefully if melting.
how to melt coarsely chop or break the chocolate into a medium heatproof bowl (a glass bowl is a good choice); place the bowl over a medium saucepan of simmering water – don't let the water touch the base of the bowl as this can overheat, and burn, the chocolate. Stir until the chocolate is smooth. Remove the chocolate from the pan immediately it is smooth to prevent it from overheating.

CINNAMON the dried inner bark of the shoots of the cinnamon tree; available in stick (quill) or ground form.
sugar a combination of ground cinnamon and caster sugar; available in the spice section of supermarkets. To make your own cinnamon sugar, combine ½ cup caster sugar and 1 teaspoon cinnamon. Store in an airtight container in the cupboard.

glossary

CLOVES dried flower buds of a tropical tree; can be used whole or in ground form. Has a strong scent and taste so should be used minimally.

COCOA POWDER also known as cocoa; dried, unsweetened, roasted then ground cocoa beans (cacao seeds).

COCONUT MACAROONS see biscuits.

CORNFLOUR also known as cornstarch; used as a thickening agent in cooking. Available as 100% maize (corn) and wheaten cornflour.

CREAM we use fresh cream, also known as pouring, single and pure cream, unless otherwise stated. It has no additives, unlike commercially thickened cream. Minimum fat content 35%.
sour a thick commercially-cultured soured cream. Minimum fat content 35%.
thickened (heavy) used as a whipping cream as it contains a thickener. Minimum fat content 35%.

EGGS some recipes in this book may call for raw or barely cooked eggs; exercise caution if there is a salmonella problem in your area. The risk is greater for those who are pregnant, elderly or very young, and those with impaired immune systems.

FLOUR
plain a general all-purpose flour made from wheat.
self-raising (rising) plain or wholemeal flour combined with baking powder in the proportion of 1 cup flour to 2 teaspoons baking powder.

GELATINE a thickening agent. Available in sheet form, known as leaf gelatine, or as a powder. Three teaspoons of dried gelatine (8g or one sachet) is roughly equivalent to four gelatine leaves.

GINGER
fresh also known as green or root ginger; the thick root of a tropical plant.
glacé fresh ginger root preserved in sugar syrup. Crystallised ginger can be substituted if rinsed with warm water and dried before using.
ground also known as powdered ginger; used as a flavouring in cakes, pies and puddings but cannot be substituted for fresh ginger.
uncrystallised may be sold as 'naked ginger' in supermarkets, is not as sweet as glacé ginger.

GLACÉ FRUIT SALAD fruit preserved in a sugar syrup. Found in health-food stores and larger supermarkets. May contain glacé pears, peaches, pineapple, apricots and citrus peel.

JELLY CRYSTALS (jello) powdered mixture of artificial fruit flavouring, gelatine and sweetener that, when mixed with water, is used to make a moulded, translucent, quivering dessert.

LAMINGTON PAN a slab cake pan 20cm x 30cm (8 inch x 12 inch), 3cm (1¼ inch) deep.

LIQUEUR we used the following liqueurs, but use your favourite brand.
cointreau citrus-flavoured.
crème de menthe peppermint-flavoured.
kirsch cherry-flavoured.
kahlua coffee-flavoured.
malibu coconut-flavoured.

MAPLE SYRUP, PURE a thin syrup distilled from the sap of the maple tree. Maple-flavoured syrup or pancake syrup is not an adequate substitute for the real thing.

MARSALA is a sweet, fortified wine. It is available in a range of styles, from sweet to dry.

MUSCATELS made by drying large muscatel grapes grown almost exclusively around Malaga in Spain. They are partially dried in the sun then drying is completed indoors; they are left on the stalk and pressed flat for sale. Muscatel is a sweet wine made from the grapes.

PASTRY READY-ROLLED SHORTCRUST a tender, crunchy, melt in the mouth buttery pastry. Once baked it is a light, crumbly easily broken short pastry. Available from the freezer section at supermarkets.

PEPPERMINT CRISP CHOCOLATE BAR a chocolate bar having a crisp peppermint centre covered with chocolate.

PISTACHIOS pale green, delicately flavoured nut inside hard off-white shells. To peel, soak shelled nuts in boiling water for about 5 minutes; drain, then pat dry with absorbent paper. Rub skins with cloth to peel.

POMEGRANATE the fruit of a large bush native to the Middle-East region, although it is now grown in other regions around the world. A dark-red, leathery-skinned fruit about the size of an orange filled with hundreds of seeds, each wrapped in an edible lucent-crimson pulp having a tangy sweet-sour flavour.

RAISINS dried sweet grapes.

REDCURRANT JELLY a preserve made from redcurrants; used as a glaze for desserts and meats, or in sauces.

RHUBARB has thick, celery-like stalks that can reach up to 60cm long; the stalks are the only edible portion of the plant – the leaves contain a toxic substance.

RICOTTA the name for this soft, white, cows-milk cheese roughly translates as 'cooked again'. It's made from whey, a by-product of other cheese-making, to which fresh milk and acid are added.

RUM the type of cask rum is aged in determines the colour of the rum. Dark rum is often aged in charred oak barrels, giving it a deep brown colour and a full flavour. White rum is aged in stainless steel tanks.

SPRINGFORM PAN a cake pan in which the side can be opened and the base removed. It is important to measure the pan when it's closed, as often the measurement that appears on the pan refers to its size when it's open.

SUGAR

brown an extremely soft, finely granulated sugar retaining molasses for its characteristic colour and flavour.

caster superfine or finely granulated table sugar.

demerara a small-grained golden sugar with a subtle molasses flavour.

icing also known as confectioners' sugar or powdered sugar; white (granulated) sugar crushed together with a small amount of cornflour.

white coarsely granulated table sugar; also known as crystal sugar.

SULTANAS dried grapes that are also known as golden raisins.

SWEETENED CONDENSED MILK a canned milk product from which 60% of the water has been removed; the remaining milk is then sweetened with sugar.

VANILLA

bean dried long, thin pod from a tropical golden orchid grown in Central and South America and Tahiti; the minuscule black seeds inside the bean are used to impart a luscious vanilla flavour.

paste made from vanilla pods and contains real seeds; one teaspoon replaces a whole vanilla pod. It is found in most supermarkets in the baking section.

extract made by extracting the flavour from the vanilla bean pod; the pods are soaked, usually in alcohol, to capture the authentic flavour. Vanilla essence is not a suitable substitute.

WHITE VINEGAR made from spirit of cane sugar.

conversion chart

measures

One Australian metric measuring cup holds approximately 250ml, one Australian metric tablespoon holds 20ml, one Australian metric teaspoon holds 5ml. The difference between one country's measuring cups and another's is within a 2- or 3-teaspoon variance, and will not affect your cooking results. North America, New Zealand and the United Kingdom use a 15ml tablespoon. All cup and spoon measurements are level. The most accurate way of measuring dry ingredients is to weigh them. When measuring liquids, use a clear glass or plastic jug with metric markings. We use large eggs with an average weight of 60g.

dry measures

METRIC	IMPERIAL
15g	½oz
30g	1oz
60g	2oz
90g	3oz
125g	4oz (¼lb)
155g	5oz
185g	6oz
220g	7oz
250g	8oz (½lb)
280g	9oz
315g	10oz
345g	11oz
375g	12oz (¾lb)
410g	13oz
440g	14oz
470g	15oz
500g	16oz (1lb)
750g	24oz (1½lb)
1kg	32oz (2lb)

liquid measures

METRIC	IMPERIAL
30ml	1 fluid oz
60ml	2 fluid oz
100ml	3 fluid oz
125ml	4 fluid oz
150ml	5 fluid oz
190ml	6 fluid oz
250ml	8 fluid oz
300ml	10 fluid oz
500ml	16 fluid oz
600ml	20 fluid oz
1000ml (1 litre)	1¾ pints

length measures

METRIC	IMPERIAL
3mm	⅛in
6mm	¼in
1cm	½in
2cm	¾in
2.5cm	1in
5cm	2in
6cm	2½in
8cm	3in
10cm	4in
13cm	5in
15cm	6in
18cm	7in
20cm	8in
23cm	9in
25cm	10in
28cm	11in
30cm	12in (1ft)

oven temperatures

These oven temperatures are only a guide for conventional ovens. For fan-forced ovens, check the manufacturer's manual.

	°C (CELSIUS)	°F (FAHRENHEIT)
Very slow	120	250
Slow	150	275-300
Moderately slow	160	325
Moderate	180	350-375
Moderately hot	200	400
Hot	220	425-450
Very hot	240	475

The imperial measurements used in these recipes are approximate only. Measurements for cake pans are approximate only. Using same-shaped cake pans of a similar size should not affect the outcome of your baking. We measure the inside top of the cake pan to determine sizes.

index

Published in 2013 by Bauer Media Books, Sydney
Bauer Media Books are published by Bauer Media Limited
54 Park St, Sydney
GPO Box 4088, Sydney, NSW 2001.
phone (02) 9282 8618; fax (02) 9126 3702
www.awwcookbooks.com.au

MEDIA GROUP

BAUER MEDIA BOOKS
Publisher - Sally Wright
Editorial & Food Director - Pamela Clark
Director of Sales, Marketing & Rights - Brian Cearnes
Creative Director - Hieu Chi Nguyen
Food Concept Director - Sophia Young

Published and Distributed in the United Kingdom by Octopus Publishing Group
Endeavour House
189 Shaftesbury Avenue
London WC2H 8JY
United Kingdom
phone (+44)(0)207 632 5400; fax (+44)(0)207 632 5405
info@octopus-publishing.co.uk;
www.octopusbooks.co.uk

Printed by 1010 Printing, China

International foreign language rights, Brian Cearnes, Bauer Media Books
bcearnes@bauer-media.com.au

A catalogue record for this book is available from the British Library.
ISBN: 978-1-74245-384-2 (paperback)

ABN 18 053 273 546